LEADERS LIKE US

GEORGIA GILMORE

BY J.P. MILLER

ILLUSTRATED BY
AMANDA QUARTEY

BAKE SALE!

Rourke
Educational Media

A Division of
Carson Dellosa Education

Before Reading: *Building Background Knowledge and Vocabulary*

Building background knowledge can help children process new information and build upon what they already know. Before reading a book, it is important to tap into what children already know about the topic. This will help them develop their vocabulary and increase their reading comprehension.

Questions and Activities to Build Background Knowledge:

1. Look at the front cover of the book and read the title. What do you think this book will be about?

2. What do you already know about this topic?

3. Take a book walk and skim the pages. Look at the table of contents, photographs, captions, and bold words. Did these text features give you any information or predictions about what you will read in this book?

Vocabulary: *Vocabulary Is Key to Reading Comprehension*

Use the following directions to prompt a conversation about each word.

- Read the vocabulary words.
- What comes to mind when you see each word?
- What do you think each word means?

> **Vocabulary Words:**
> - boycott
> - donate
> - fundraising
> - landmark
> - manage
> - revenue
> - segregated
> - volunteer

During Reading: *Reading for Meaning and Understanding*

To achieve deep comprehension of a book, children are encouraged to use close reading strategies. During reading, it is important to have children stop and make connections. These connections result in deeper analysis and understanding of a book.

 Close Reading a Text

During reading, have children stop and talk about the following:

- Any confusing parts
- Any unknown words
- Text to text, text to self, text to world connections
- The main idea in each chapter or heading

Encourage children to use context clues to determine the meaning of any unknown words. These strategies will help children learn to analyze the text more thoroughly as they read.

When you are finished reading this book, turn to the next-to-last page for **Text-Dependent Questions** and an **Extension Activity**.

TABLE OF CONTENTS

COMMITTEE OF ONE 4

USE WHAT YOU GOT 8

MY HOUSE IS YOUR HOUSE 14

TIME LINE 21

GLOSSARY 22

INDEX 23

TEXT-DEPENDENT QUESTIONS....................... 23

EXTENSION ACTIVITY.................................... 23

ABOUT THE AUTHOR
AND ILLUSTRATOR 24

COMMITTEE OF ONE

Have you ever wanted to be a **volunteer**? Where would you go to help? What skills do you have? Georgia Gilmore loved to cook. She used her cooking skills to help fund the Montgomery Bus **Boycott**. She was a leader in **fundraising**.

Hot grease sizzled. Georgia put the last drumstick into the hot skillet. She was a great soul food cook. Fried chicken, macaroni and cheese, cakes, and pies were her best dishes.

Georgia sold her food at hair salons and barbershops. Her fried chicken and fish dinners were top sellers. She raised a lot of money.

Georgia never paid herself one penny. At the end of the day, she split the money into two piles. One pile was to buy more food and supplies. The other she gave to Civil Rights leaders for the Montgomery Bus Boycott.

A DAY IN GEORGIA GILMORE'S SHOES
A typical day started at 4:00 a.m. with Georgia preparing for lunch. The menu changed daily but always included fried fish or chicken, stuffed pork chops, potato salad, collards, black-eyed peas, yams, and bread pudding.

When asked where the money came from, Georgia jokingly said, "It came from nowhere."

She was a committee of one. Her club? The Club from Nowhere.

USE WHAT YOU GOT

A crowd was outside the Holt Street Baptist Church. There was no more room inside. The pews were full, and people stood against the walls. The day-long bus boycott was a success. Everyone was there to hear Dr. Martin Luther King Jr. He had a new plan of action.

Georgia looked around. She was glad she left work early. She got a good seat. She would have no problem hearing Dr. King.

Dr. King wanted to hit the city where it hurt most: their **revenue**. In order to create social change, the boycott had to run longer. He didn't want to stop until the buses were no longer **segregated**. He warned that it would take a lot of volunteers and money for his plan to work.

Georgia was ready to help however she could. Ushers passed the offering basket. People put money in. It was a good start, but not enough. Dr. King asked everyone to use their own skills to help. They would need people to drive since they were boycotting the bus. They would need people to stay behind with children while adults went to protests. And they would need more money. The community answered.

Drivers drove...

babysitters sat with children...

cooks cooked.

Whatever was needed...members of the Black community could do it.

Georgia liked what Dr. King said. She knew exactly what she would do to help. Cook! She would sell her food and **donate** the money to the boycott.

MY HOUSE IS YOUR HOUSE

Georgia had been mistreated by a white bus driver before. He took her fare and drove off before she could get on the bus. Georgia never forgot about it. That clash pushed her to help. That driver had messed with the wrong lady.

Georgia's boss didn't like her being involved in the boycott. She was fired from her job as a chef. She didn't care. It gave her more time to **manage** the Club from Nowhere. She grew the club from one to over forty members. They sold food all over, in places such as beauty shops and churches. Georgia picked up the money they raised and dropped it off at the Holt Street Baptist Church. Her donations were crucial to keeping the boycott going. The boycott lasted for 381 days.

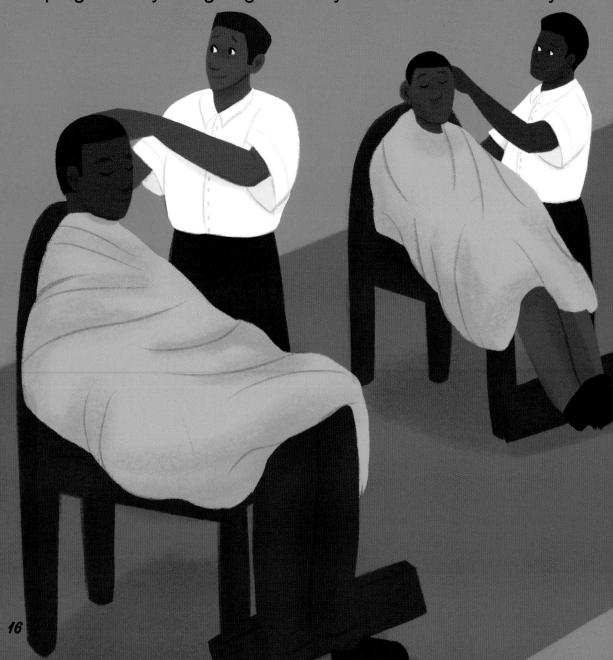

Dr. King loved Georgia's food. He urged her to open her own restaurant. Georgia thought that was a great idea. She turned her living room into a dining area. Her house was her restaurant. It was everybody's house, and everyone was welcome. Dr. King and other Civil Rights leaders went there to eat and have meetings.

SPIRITED GEORGIA

Georgia Gilmore was fiery at times. She and Dr.
Martin Luther King Jr. became good friends. He
nicknamed her "Tiny." Georgia credited Dr. King
for helping her learn to control her temper.

Georgia Gilmore stayed active in Civil Rights. She was part of a class action lawsuit to integrate public parks in Montgomery. Georgia died on March 9, 1990, while cooking for people marching to celebrate the 25th anniversary of the march from Selma to Montgomery. In 1995, the state of Alabama designated her home as a national **landmark**.

" Some Negroes could not afford to stick out their necks more than others because they had independent incomes, but some just couldn't afford to be called 'ring leaders' and have the white folks fire them. So when we made our financial reports to the MIA officers we had them record us as the money coming from nowhere. 'The Club from Nowhere.' —Georgia Gilmore "

TIME LINE

1920 Georgia Gilmore is born February 5th in Montgomery, Alabama.

1955 Georgia experiences unfair treatment from a white bus driver.

1955 Georgia attends the first mass meeting of the Montgomery Improvement Association (MIA) at the Holt Street Baptist Church on December 5th.

1955 Georgia is fired from her job as a chef at the National Lunch Company for participating in the Civil Rights Movement.

1955–56 Georgia organizes the Club from Nowhere to cook and sell food, giving all of the proceeds to the MIA to fund the Montgomery Bus Boycott.

1957 Georgia turns her home into a restaurant and starts a catering business.

1958 Georgia is part of a class action lawsuit to desegregate public parks in Montgomery, Alabama.

1990 Georgia dies on March 9th while preparing food for marchers commemorating the 25th anniversary of the march from Selma to Montgomery.

1995 Alabama designates Georgia's home a national landmark.

GLOSSARY

boycott (BOI-kaht): to refuse to do business with someone as a punishment or protest

donate (DOH-nate): to give something to a charity or a cause

fundraising (FUHND-rayz-ing): raising money for a cause

landmark (LAND-mahrk): a building or place picked and pointed out as important

manage (MAN-ij): to be in charge of a business or process

revenue (REV-uh-noo): the money the government gets from taxes and other sources, such as public transportation

segregated (SEG-ri-gate-id): the act of keeping groups separated and apart

volunteer (vah-luhn-TEER): a person who offers to do a job without pay

INDEX

Civil Rights 6, 18, 20

class action lawsuit 20

Club from Nowhere 7, 16,
    20

fare 15

integrate 20

Montgomery Bus Boycott 4,
    6

skills 4, 13

ushers 13

TEXT-DEPENDENT QUESTIONS

1. What was the Montgomery Bus Boycott?

2. How did the community rise up to help keep the Montgomery Bus Boycott going?

3. Why did Georgia Gilmore name her club *The Club from Nowhere?*

4. What class action lawsuit was Georgia Gilmore involved in?

5. Who suggested Georgia Gilmore open her own restaurant?

EXTENSION ACTIVITY

Throw a giving party. Contact a nonprofit organization where you live such as a food pantry, homeless shelter, assisted living center, etc. Ask your guests to bring items to be donated. Box the items up and deliver them to the nonprofit organization. Helping others will make you feel so good inside!

ABOUT THE AUTHOR

J.P. Miller Growing up, J.P. Miller loved reading stories that she could become immersed in. As a writer, she enjoys doing the same for her readers. Through the gift of storytelling, she is able to bring little- and well-known people and events in African American history to life for young readers. She hopes that her stories will augment the classroom experience and inspire her readers. J.P. lives in metro Atlanta and is the author of the *Careers in the US Military* and *Black Stories Matter* series. J.P. is the winner of the 2021 Black Authors Matter Award sponsored by the National Black Book Festival.

ABOUT THE ILLUSTRATOR

Amanda Quartey Amanda lives in the UK and was born and bred in London. She has always loved to draw and has been doing so ever since she can remember. At the age of 14, she moved to Ghana and studied art in school. She later returned to the UK to study graphic design. Her artistic path deviated slightly when she studied Classics at her university. Over the years, in a bid to return to her artistic roots, Amanda has built a professional illustration portfolio and is now loving every bit of her illustration career.

© 2022 Rourke Educational Media

www.rourkeeducationalmedia.com

Quote source: Nadasen, Premillia, "Georgia Gilmore, Overlooked Activist of Montgomery Bus Boycott," Beacon Press, March 18, 2016: Georgia Gilmore, Overlooked Activist of the Montgomery Bus Boycott - Beacon Broadside: A Project of Beacon Press

Edited by: Hailey Scragg
Illustrations by: Amanda Quartey
Cover and interior layout by: J.J. Giddings

Library of Congress PCN Data

Georgia Gilmore / J.P. Miller
(Leaders Like Us)
ISBN 978-1-73165-180-8 (hard cover)
ISBN 978-1-73165-225-6 (soft cover)
ISBN 978-1-73165-195-2 (e-Book)
ISBN 978-1-73165-210-2 (ePub)
Library of Congress Control Number: 2021944577

Rourke Educational Media
Printed in the United States of America
01-3402111937